WE'VE GOT PERSONALITY
NOW WHAT!

We've Got Personality Now What!

K.L. Fischer PhD

K.L. Fischer Publications

Publisher: K.L. Fischer Publications

ISBN-13: 978-1534890237

ISBN-10: 1534890238

Table of Contents

I. Early Development Of Personality Through Person Perception And Self-Experience

Everybody's got one. Everybody's born with one. Some would say we've got one even before we're born. Everyone's is different. No two are exactly alike. Even if we could be cloned, they'd still be different. Each one is unique, distinctive, one of a kind. It stays with us our entire life. From our first breath to our last. Its beginning is basic and rudimentary. It slowly develops over time. Some of it is genetic but most of it is acquired.

What am I talking about? I'm talkin' personality = That which distinguishes us as a person. It's what we perceive when we perceive a person. It's what we perceive when we perceive ourselves. Who am I? I am who I am. You want to get to know me, you need to get to know my personality. To get to know my personality, you need to get to know me. I, of course, am more than my personality. I am a personality? No. I have a personality. I am a person with a personality.

One gets to know the other's personality through Person Perception – interacting with, relating to, experiencing your Self with their Self. One's personality develops through person perception and self-experience. The way this works is that the child gets a pretty good idea of what their personality is like from perceiving the way their parents, or parent substitutes, teachers, relatives, friends perceive them. From the other's facial expression, mannerisms, gestures, voice tone, voice content, when the other either is reacting to their presentation or they are reacting to the other's presentation. When a person perception takes place it's a function of a presenter and a perceiver. When the perceiver reacts to the other's presentation, their reaction becomes a presentation for the other to perceive, and react to, and so on.

A child learns early on, especially if they have a demonstrative parent, when what they're doing the parent likes or not. If the parent doesn't like it, they let the child know. How? Quite often by **what** they say and **how** they say it. "What are you doing? Stop that, before you break something." The voice tone accompanying the words is harsh, loud, and commanding. Then there's the frowning, non-smiling face to go along with it, and the few steps forward, arms extended.

All of these perceptual cues combine to give the child a percept that what they're doing the parent doesn't like. That they could very well be angry with them. That they could be in trouble. That there may be some sort of punishment forthcoming. If the parent is relatively consistent in the way they react to the child's doing something they don't like, then when the child does other things the parent doesn't like, the child can anticipate the parent having a similar reaction.

The perception that the child's presentation will elicit a similar reaction from the parent (as before) may become a deterrent to proceed the next time and become a precipitator for behavioral change. This is how the personality of the child gets shaped and molded. They do something the parent doesn't like. They get the treatment as described above.

Ah, but let's turn things around and allow for the fact that even with serendipity the child will come upon a behavior that the parent likes. When this occurs, let's hope the demonstrative parent will be presenting perceptual cues to the child that they will perceive as a positive well-pleased response – comprised of a smiling face, a soft, gentle, welcoming tone with approving reinforcing words to match. The probability of the child repeating same or similar behaviors goes up dramatically. Staying away from displeasing behavior and pursuing instead parent-pleasing behavior will result in the need to please rising in the child's hierarchy of needs and pleaser will become an important characteristic in the child's personality.

Other than by serendipity, the child learns behaviors, non-verbal and verbal, by perceiving other siblings behave in a way that gets a favorable response and then emulating that same behavior. Sometimes this works and sometimes it doesn't. Sometimes the parent responds more favorably to the behavior of one child than the other even though their behaviors are pretty much the same. This seemingly preferential treatment of the one over the other may at first confuse the child who tried to emulate the other's behavior. What's up with this? The other does it and the parent responds like it was something special.

When the one follows after with the same behavior – it's no big deal. As a matter of fact – it's no deal at all.

A fertile context for sibling rivalry to grow. I've seen this phenomenon time and again when there are two children of the same sex, a couple of years apart. It starts out with the younger trying to emulate the older to get some of those positive rewarding parental responses. But for whatever reason, maybe because the parent has seen it before, or maybe because the child trying to duplicate the other's performance comes up short in some way or another – Whatever – The parent's response from the child's perspective leaves much to be desired.

An extension of this phenomenon is then that the second child heads off in another direction. If emulating the other's behavior doesn't seem to work, the child begins to explore and experiment with their own set of behaviors. Some of these new behaviors work in the sense that they get favorable responses. Some of them don't and this the child finds out the hard way. [Thus the comments based on observations and perception – "My two boys (two girls) couldn't be more different – Their personalities are totally opposite."]

Birth order is an important variable as one's personality develops through person perception and self-experience . . . The older (oldest, whatever the case) child doesn't necessarily have it made. Let's get rid of that idea. Remember, for the parents this is the first time through. They are learning as they go along. They make mistakes. They inadvertently reinforce undesirable behaviors and fail to reinforce desirable behaviors in a way to keep them coming. They exert too little control regarding some behaviors – Too much control regarding others.

The first child usually turns out to be more adult-oriented (as does an only child). The first child tries hard to please. To do the right thing. To make their parents proud. The key words here are "tries hard." If not successful, measured by their perception of their parents' perception of them, they could stop trying. Give up. Become depressed. Or, go off in an entirely different direction from what their parents envisioned for them.

This presents the second child an opening if they wish to take it. Up to the point where the first child gets off track the second child had it made. While the first child was trying hard to do their best, the second child could relax and do their thing, get rambunctious from time to time with few repercussions, if any. But now if the second child chooses to replace the first child and take their position "on the train" upholding family tradition, the trade-off will be that the second child will have to cool their behaviors some and stay steady as they go and drop some of their past shenanigans.

As long as we're talking about birth-order effects on personality, let's not forget the common plight of the middle child. If the middle child is the same gender as the one on either side, "You can forget about it" – That is precisely what tends to happen – The middle child is often forgotten about. Typically, the older child and the younger child draw more attention. The middle child sort of plods along on their own. Relatively unnoticed. Pretty much carving out their own identity. Unobtrusively going about their business while remaining in the background.

It's worth noting that in the case where all three children are of the same gender, the middle child may mature in being able to be on their own and hold their own sooner than the other two. However, when the middle child is flanked by two of the other gender, then very little of what I've said about the middle child pertains. The reality that they are the only one of their gender makes a big difference in neutralizing whatever short-fall the before-mentioned middle child experienced.

The youngest child (as the only child also experiences) is in a class by themselves. Makes sense. By this time parents have had plenty of practice. They've learned what works and doesn't work. There's usually a consensus among siblings that the youngest "gets all the gravy" and that even the strictest and sternest of parents has mellowed (at least a little bit) by this time.

A personal note . . . My kid sister came along thirteen years after I did and nineteen years after my older sister. My sister (my younger one) had a different mother but the same father. Maybe because both parents were her birth parents she was treated preferentially. Being the youngest by so many years I'm sure helped as well. Her relation with our father was day and night different than with us – other two. She got to talk at the supper table, even joke around with my father and even laugh in his presence. My older sister and I when we were kids were stone silent, hurrying to get through the ordeal. We never thought of joking with our father and laughing (you could forget about that). That part – No laughing – was no great loss because eating supper precisely at 4:45 when my father came home from work, with the no nonsense stern demeanor of our father permeating the room was no laughing matter in the first place.

But let's get back to talking about "child in general." The single most important variable in determining the child's personality development derives from the child's perception of how their parents perceive them. The child's perception of their parents' perception of them becomes for all intents and purposes the way the child subsequently perceives themselves.

The child is trying to learn something new – A new behavior they haven't tried before. Keeping it simple, let's say the new behavior is – Making their bed. Right off the bat I don't see this behavior gender specific – that just boys should learn to do it ☺. You're starting to get my point. Remember, parents are models. Both parents. For both genders.

Now then, in teaching your child to make their bed, you first let them observe you doing it. Answer whatever questions they might have about the mechanics of the job. Do not answer the question . . . Why do I have to make my own bed?

Next, let them give it a try under your tutelage and guide them as they do it. Make suggestions in a helping manner and let them have another go at it. Be patient, Stay calm. If the second attempt is better than the first, say so. If not, show them one more time where they can improve. After this, they're on their own. Make It clear to them that you expect them to make their bed from here on in. When you check on the job they've done, first reinforce the effort, even if the job isn't done as well as you would have liked. Show them where they could still improve. But under no circumstances expect perfection (which could mean your perception of how you would do it.)

The key thing in all of this is that when our child is learning a new behavior – We show them how to do it. Observe them trying to do it. Support their effort. Offer suggestions. Encourage questions. Let them try it a couple of times. Then, if we see they're catching on, we build on that and then let them do it on their own. If it's a behavior involving a daily activity (I don't like the word "chore" it has a negative sound to it), and our child commits to doing it – and does it faithfully – and meets our standard for our child (reduced a standard deviation of one or two from our own) we have helped our child attain a sense of Responsibility, Accomplishment, Commitment. – All these good things add up to an increase in self-worth.

One could think of it this way – As parents we ask ourselves the question – What kind of person would we like our child to be? – What kind of personality would we like our child to have? Even if it were possible, we wouldn't want our child to be just like we are – Now, would we? Aren't there things about our personality we really don't like? If we lower our defenses and trust our perceptions – Then look at the picture of ourselves objectively – What characteristics do we see we would like to have more of, less of – Or, what would we like to have that we don't have yet (as far as we know)? I'm hoping you, my reader, get actively involved in doing this exercise – I.e. summarily looking at some characteristics you don't like about yourself – Those you do like – Those you think you would like if you should discover them in yourselves.

The other thing for you to do would be to validate how well – or how poorly – your perspective of yourself matches up with the other's perception of you. Let's say one of the things you like about yourself is that you're a **kind** person. Your other agrees. It fits with their perception of you. This is a characteristic you would like to see in your child. Your other agrees. By the kind way you talk to your other, your child, your extended family, your friends, even to those you may not know. By your acts of **kindness** to those who need a hand, you are presenting the perceptional cue of kindness. Your child is watching and listening and learning from you what kind behaviors, verbal and non-verbal, look and sound like. You're showing your child – Kindness is not a gender thing – It's a person thing.

You, the parent, will also be watching and listening – perceiving your child with your eyes and ears – looking for perceptual cues that your child is discovering this **kindness** thing. – You see it in the way they treat the family pet. In the way they look out for their friend. In the kindness they show a sibling. In the kind act they do for their parents. The characteristic, kindness (they now are manifesting) – watching and listening to you, the parent, had a lot to do with their obtaining it. Don't miss an opportunity – if you can help it – to recognize, acknowledge, and positively reinforce the words and acts of kindness emanating from your child. You want this acquired characteristic to become a mainstay in your child's personality.

I'm sure there are other characteristics you would like to see in your child's personality – Positive qualities like: Responsibleness. Trustworthiness. Loyalty. Caring. Tenderness. Strength of Character. Truthfulness. Dependability. Resourcefulness.

Gentleness. Respectfulness (I'm sure you could add to this list). Their life is a process that has no end until they are no more. We parents try to sow the seed and water it and do our best to keep it growing – Until it can make it on its own – Not really on its own because it doesn't want to be alone – It wants to be with another in a reciprocal relationship helping each other grow.

These are positive qualities we would hope to have growing in our personality – That our children may pick them up from us. But reality says there may be negative qualities in us as well. These it would be good for us to change for all our sakes. For example, **Quick to Anger** is a characteristic some of us have in our personality. It gets us into trouble. We say or do things we later regret. We hurt other's feelings with our words. We scare others with our tone and our menacing mannerisms. We drive people away. They don't want to be with us, when we're like this. This would be an example of a personality characteristic we would like to have far less of. Our father or mother may have been (or maybe still are) – Quick to anger. We see it in them. We don't like it. We see it in ourselves. We don't like it. We may see it in our children and don't like it.

The change must begin with us. If we truly want to help our child modify their personality characteristic of reactive anger – we must start with ourselves. If we are able to take control of our anger – (the precursor of which is usually frustration – or a feeling that things are out of our control) by becoming aware earlier in the process of how things are building up within us – And tell ourselves to stay calm – Take it easy – We'll get through this – We can modify this characteristic we have too much of.

Our other, our child, our parents, the other's parents, fellow workers, friends – given time (since by now they have acquired a predisposed perceptual set of us) will begin to change the way they perceive us. This will change the way we perceive they perceive us – And the way we perceive ourselves. We'll regress now and then and slip into our old behavior, but it will be temporary. We'll own it. Apologize for it. Announce we'll try harder. Then follow up with doing better.

An interesting phenomenon to me is how characteristics in our personality can intermesh with needs. Using quick to anger as the characteristic, the **Need to Control** one's physical and human environment comes to mind. Usually the person having a personality with a large need to control is also a person who has difficulty discriminating between what they can control and what they can't. This inability to discriminate only adds to their frustration. Sometimes their need to control flies into the face of reality. They keep trying but they're spinning their wheels – going nowhere and getting hotter and hotter under the collar. [A classic example of how the need to control elicits anger.]

II. Diagnosing A Personality Disorder

At this point I need to give you some background before I go on to talk to you about personality tendencies and how they fit into the scheme of things. First of all, you should know that I am not only a reality therapist but also call myself a "**Personologist.**" I specialize in treating **Personality Disorders** (Disorders of the Personality). [You should also know that there are psychiatrists and psychologists who scoff at the mention of personality disorders and don't believe there are such things.]

The Diagnostic Manual psychiatrists and psychologists use to make their diagnoses includes Personality Disorders. Moreover, when we make a diagnosis we use Five Axes: On Axis I go mood disorders like anxiety, depression, adjustment disorders, dissociative disorders (You get the picture). Axis II is where personality disorders belong. I include personality tendencies on this Axis when my diagnosis falls short of a full-blown personality disorder (I'll explain all of this later). This, unfortunately, is the Axis that gets the least attention from many of my colleagues. For me it is just the opposite – I see Axis I stuff emanating from Axis II stuff. My colleagues disagree.

To complete the diagnosis – Axis III considers physical symptoms. Axis IV speaks to the area or context in which the client is having the most trouble functioning (work, home, social situations, school etc.). Axis V asks the therapist to assign a numerical value to the level at which the therapist perceives the client to be functioning. As a clinical supervisor of therapists (starting out) I insisted they not ignore Axis II. I wanted them to consider the client's personality tendencies. I really didn't expect them to diagnose a full-blown personality disorder. They'd have to consult with me before they came to that conclusion.

My PhD is in Personality Psychology. My area of expertise doing psychotherapy is in treating Personality Disorders. My doctoral research had to do with Person Perception. Let's say I perceive my client's personality using the four aspects of person perception: Appearance, Facial expression, Mannerisms, How they say, What they say. I perceive my client as a high achiever. I know there are basically two classes of high achievers – One, with a large need to succeed – The other with a large need to avoid failure. I perceive my client to fit the latter category.

My client who happens to be in their first year in college presents like they are rubber band tight. They are constantly fidgeting. They look like they haven't been getting enough sleep. They report they have a major exam coming up which will account for fifty percent of their grade. So on Axis I, I'm thinking (at the very least) a diagnosis of Adjustment Disorder with Anxious Mood. When I'm thinking Adjustment Mood, I'm thinking more episodic than chronic. However if the anxiety my client is displaying is not specific to academic performance (If it were taking-an-exam-specific, we'd be looking at Test Anxiety) but shows up in other areas (Axis IV Stuff) wherever and whenever there is the need to do well, I'm now thinking Psychoneurotic Anxiety Disorder – or even Generalized Anxiety.

The Axis II stuff is the key to my understanding what's going on with my client – That they get so anxious when the pressure's on to do well and be successful. At this stage in my client's life much of the pressure they're experiencing is self-imposed. Early in my client's life this wasn't the case – That the pressure and the anxiety that came with it was self-imposed. On the contrary. It would be more perceptually valid to say – Then, it was other-imposed. Remember our self-concept i.e. our picture of ourself from early on is painted by the perceptions we have of how others perceive us. In my client's case, very early on, it was made very clear by their parents whose philosophy was – If it's worth doing at all, it's worth doing well. They preached being very thorough – Very careful so as not to make any mistakes. Mistakes attributed to haste, carelessness (especially when one knew the answer) were particularly irksome to them. When they viewed the finished work – Be it homework or a test corrected, brought home from school – Their eyes flew to the red marks (even though in the scheme of things they were few and far between). The overall product of work – though very well done – elicited not more than a guarded grunt of approval.

The key difference between the two kinds of high achievers, one having a large need to succeed – the other a large need to avoid failure – derives from the differential way the parents of each treated their success and/or failure. The parents, of the second kind, were neutral toward success and punished failure. [High achievers with a large need to succeed had parents who positively reinforced success but were neutral toward failure.] The dynamic I'm centering on here is the interaction between parents and children in which perceptual cues are given and received by both parties resulting in personality tendencies being strengthened or reduced, or in some cases, all but extinguished.

Lest those of you who have no children are feeling overlooked – Know that all of this has relevance since all of us once were children. Our parents presented perceptual cues to us giving us a picture of what they wanted from us. That picture became our picture of ourselves. Our observable behaviors became perceptual cues for them to see whether the picture of ourselves they presented to us and the picture of ourselves we presented back to them were essentially in accord.

As adults we have brought the picture our parents had of us – as children – with us. Some changes have been made, but mostly small ones – Which is to say personalities don't really change that much over time. Some of our characteristics we've added to – Some we've subtracted from – A few may be new (since we were a child) but only a few. Our perceptible personality tendencies tend to stand the test of time. Part of this has to do, I'm sure, with the perceptual reality that personality tendencies are probably the most observable and "standoutish" part of our personality. In addition, a personality tendency may manifest itself in a multiplicity and diversity of observable behaviors. Take for example the personality tendency of **Competitiveness** and visualize the many different situations in which observable behaviors stemming from this personality tendency might potentially show up. This surely could be one of those personality tendencies – if left unchecked – could easily become a dominant force in one's personality. [I bet some of my readers – either yourself – or your other – can relate.]

Conceivably the personality tendency of competitiveness could team up (as it were) with the personality **Need To Strive For Perfection** (or to be

Number One). The reality that no matter how good you are at something – someone is always better – could have a crushing effect on one who strives to be the best – Or, in their reality has to be the best. To take this one step further – The personality tendency of competitiveness plus the personality need to be the best could add up to the person walking away from a sport (if that were what we're talking about) – If they didn't come out on top. And if their response were to walk away from a sport that (up to now) they loved – Can depression be far behind? I think not [Axis I stuff = Situational Depression].

For another example, let's use the personality tendency of being **Hypercritical**. Let's combine this with the personality need **To Do things Right** – Themselves. And have others do things right ("Right" – meaning what the person perceiving decides is right). Consider the multifaceted fallout for this person . . . The constant pressure of doing or saying things right – One can never let down. The compulsion which drives the person to point out to the other where they went wrong (occurring during, or, after the fact) – The perfect way to lose friends and estrange people. [The high cost of having to be right and having to show others where they're wrong is to be shunned and avoided and chosen last. And lastly, don't be surprised if we have still another candidate for Episodic Depression (Axis I stuff).]

The personality tendency of **Self Control** can combine with the personality need **To Control Self** so that when the person's life is out of control the person may strive to get their life back in control i.e. self control – This could very well be a paradigm for developing an Eating Disorder – The Eating Disorder untreated can have serious physical and psychological consequences for the person.

The diagnosis on Axis I of **Social Anxiety** may stem from a conflict between wanting interpersonal contact but being reluctant to do so because of being afraid of criticism, disapproval or rejection. This is an example of an approach-avoidance conflict which by its very push-pull nature generates anxiety. Defenses rise to protect one from the true picture of one's Self. Anxiety is lessened by avoidance at the cost of non-involvement.

What I do in psychotherapy is develop my own picture of my client's picture of themselves. I try to get them to tell me how they see themselves. I ask them to describe their personality. If I'm seeing a couple individually, I ask each to describe the other's personality as well. This way I get their perception of themselves and their perception of their other. I ask each of them one more thing – How each perceives the other perceives them.

I validate their perceptions of themselves and other's with my own. [I keep my perceptions to myself (at first) and then when I think the time is right, I share mine – individually, with each of them.] If what I see is pretty much in keeping with what they see, i.e. both of us see personality tendencies and needs that are unique to their person – These then are what each of them brings to a given situation and become an integral part of each other's presentation and perception.

III. Using You My Reader As An Example

Permit me to use you my reader as an example. I'm treating you, individually – [Not as part of a couple in therapy with me, however.] I'm listening intently to what you have to say. I'm also paying attention to how you're saying what you're saying. I'm perceiving your facial expressions and your mannerisms as well. As you give me your self-report (including what prompted you to see me) and reiterate what's been happening in your life – you start to talk about your other and the relationship you have with each other. You tell me you love your other dearly, but lately (I find out later we're talking about the last six months) you have felt a distance growing between the two of you. It seems every time you've tried to get close, you've been turned away by one excuse after the other. It's been more than six months since you had sex. Come to think about it – it's been longer than that since you even touched each other.

Of course, all the time you're telling me your story – I'm perceiving what you're presenting. I'm especially noting any nuances of change in your presentation. For instance, I notice when you talk specifically about your other – how you love the other dearly – Your face got softer, as did your tone. When you spoke of the distance between you two – Your face got sad. When you talked about no sex for the past six months – You looked and sounded frustrated. When you told me about no touching going on for an even longer time – You looked and sounded discouraged. The content of your words, however, gave me a perception that you missed more than the sex. You missed the closeness. This (as your therapist) gave me a perception of you – That you would be more open to the insights I would be giving and the suggestions I would be making to you about what you might do to bring about more closeness in your relationship.

In perceiving you in subsequent sessions – I'm getting a picture of your personality tendencies and needs. I see you as a person with passive tendencies and a need to have the other take the initiative – If anything of closeness is going to happen between the two of you. Of course, you also have a larger fear of rejection than is normal. So on Axis I there's some anxiety there involving closeness and the possibility of withdrawal and depression if perceptions and behaviors don't change.

Condensing six months of therapy with you into a few paragraphs – Here's how I would proceed with you. First of all, an assumption would have to be made that through your self-report and one session with your other (I try to see the other once to get a firsthand perception), I now have a pretty good idea of what your other's personality is like – How your other perceives you – How they think you perceive them, and how they perceive themselves. This is where thirty-five years of perceiving people's personalities comes in – Clients have said to me at our very first session – You must have met my other before – Sounds like you know them better than I do. Of course, I haven't met their other yet. I've only had their self-report and my perception of their other through them to work with. After I've had my one and only session with their other – I'm able to validate my prior second-hand perceptions and find them to be quite accurate.

The insights I would be giving you, in this instance, would be for you to become less passive and more proactive. The hesitancy – The holding back – The waiting until you're sure – Needing signs of encouragement before you make the first move – All of these behaviors have got to go. However, lest your other perceive you as having only sex on your mind – try other forms of closeness as well. Systematically desensitize yourself, and the other, with successive approximations which will help mitigate anxieties around closeness – In other words, gradually work up to it. Between you and me and the fence post – This is what the other has been looking for – But were themselves anxious about what might happen if they asserted it. [Ironic, to say the least – both not asserting – both being anxious about rejection]. The prognosis for your relationship's Chances – or should we rather say – Changes-For-More-Closeness – is good to excellent – If you are able to become more assertive and temper it with sensitivity.

Can you see now how important identifying personality tendencies and needs is in the diagnosis, treatment, and prognosis facets of the psychotherapeutic process! To help you help yourselves (apart from psychotherapy) I propose you engage in the following paradigm for self-analysis . . . First of all, perceive yourself – Meaning, take an objective realistic look at your Self. Look especially for personality tendencies and needs. [By now I'm sure you know what I'm talking about – But just in case, here's one more time. For example, Personality Tendency = To be a care-giver. Personality Need = To be in control. Presentation = I'll take care of you. Price = I will need to be the one in control. Attracts those looking to be taken care of, but on the other hand don't want to be controlled.] The relationship problem that usually arises is the care-giver gets tired of doing all the giving – and getting mixed messages from the other in return – "I like your care-giving but don't like the control that comes with it."

It's our personality tendencies and needs that manifest themselves in our presentation and correspondingly effect the way we are perceived. If my personality tendency is **Conscientiousness** and my personality need is to **Not Overlook Any Detail** – it's not difficult to predict how I will present myself and how I will be perceived. This will receive mixed reviews in the workplace depending upon the perceiver's bias re thoroughness or quickness (if the presenter doesn't have both). If thoroughness is the ticket – both the presenter and perceiver should be satisfied.

Look at your own personality tendencies and needs and see How well – How so-so – How poorly – they fit what you wish to present and how you wish to be perceived. It may depend on what area of your life (Axis IV stuff) we're talking about. Your presentation may work very well for you at your job. But at home, with your other (especially if your other is short on patience) your presentation may be problematic. [See how important personality and person perception are to our figuring out – What about the picture we have of ourselves we wish to leave pretty much as is – What parts we would like to enhance or reduce – What parts we don't yet see so we don't know how we'll feel about those (if and when they do appear).]

IV. Personality Tendencies And Personality Needs Some Of Us Have

Consider the personality tendency some of us have, **To Be Devoted To Work**; and the personality need **To Produce At A High Level**. These two personality variables combine to leave such a one with little quantity of time to spend with loved ones. And the quality of that time is usually hampered by a lack of energy (already spent elsewhere). There's almost no time at all left over for leisure activities and friendships. The rationalization usually presented in a case like this is that the one perceives themselves as having no other choice. They view the situation solely as a have-to. [This, even when objective reality would present no obvious economic necessity.] Perhaps two other personality needs are in effect here – the **Need To Excel**; the **Need Not To Fail** – and these then become the driving force behind devotion to – and high level productivity at – work. [Sounds like we might be talking about a Workaholic here.] If we take a perceptual snapshot of this person's self-concept – i.e. the picture they present to themselves – We will see that a substantial portion of that picture presents the person at work. And we'll conclude (rightly so) that a substantial portion of the person's self-worth rides on the perpetuation of that picture.

Another personality tendency and personality need my clients have presented are – The tendency – **Dependency** – and the **Need to Overlap Relationships** (or, if not overlap – give themselves **little if any time between relationships**). I often get to see them after a close relationship has ended and they've already begun another one. [Bottom line is their need for empathy, care, and support has triggered their impulsive side. Often they and their brand-new-other have come from having similar experiences.]

I say to myself (first) and to my client (later) how I wish they had come to me before they had started another relationship. The rebound effect is alive, but not often well. If my client has been the Dumpee – they're hurt and then angry. If my client was the Dumper – they're angry and then hurt. [Sometimes the end is mutually agreed upon – However, there remains a sense of loss, disappointment, sadness]

Vulnerability is the word of the days and nights. The caveat I give (if I get the chance before my client leaps) would be – Take your time. Don't be in a hurry. Take the opportunity now that you're on your own – to learn more about yourself, your personality tendencies and needs. Find a therapist if you don't already have one. You need their help in order to look at yourself objectively and realistically. They'll help you discover what kind of personalities you attract and what kind you gravitate toward. All of this is to give you time to – Recover, discover, inquire, vent – Get empathy, insights, support for making behavioral changes – Change perceptions of yourselves and others – Practice presenting and perceiving. All of this is necessary – Lest you repeat yourself (unbeknownst to you, and quite possibly the other).

Some of my clients, over the years, have presented the personality tendency of **Grandiosity** – a personality need to **Exaggerate Their Achievements And Talents**. [An interesting sidebar to this is that even as they think and present in grandiose terms – In their self-report they disclose, perhaps unknowingly, information that underscores their ordinariness.] Their presentation is a mixture of how they perceive themselves – their perception of other's perceptions of them – and their perception of others.

The way they perceive themselves is more a wish than a reality. What's missing perceptually in their presentation is the cue of conviction in their voice tone. The content of the words that follow is filled with hedges and qualifiers. Their perception of their future is not substantiated by their past or present. Their defenses are high. Their flight pattern at present is low. But because of their grandiose thinking it's hard to ground them.

Then there are clients whose personality tendency is **Hypersensitivity** – and personality need **To Go Slowly and Proceed Cautiously With Regard To Having Close Relationships**. Fears of being shamed or ridiculed are behind their hesitancy. Close encounters subject both parties to perceptual scrutiny. Mutual trust is a prerequisite for personal exposure. Trust, by my definition, is an exchange of vulnerability without either taking advantage of the other. Feeling of inadequacy is the backdrop for hypersensitivity. The hypersensitive person is supersensitive to the perceptual cues given off by others to their presentation. When I have one of these as my client I am perpetually giving my client alternative perceptual interpretations to the perceptions they have of others' perceptions of them. I wish they were able to validate for themselves how the other perceives them – Rather than, as they are prone to do – project onto the other negative perceptions of themselves – which could very well not be there.

"My Way or the Highway" is the motto of a person with a personality tendency of **Self-Righteousness** – a personality need **That Others Submit to Exactly their Way Of Doing Things**. This authoritarian approach usually means that one has a hard time working with others or delegating tasks and that their defenses are high to preserve their image of not making a mistake. [Since everyone is eventually bound to make one – When they do – it comes down hard on them]

Then there's the person whose personality tendency is to **Volunteer To Do Things Unpleasant** because their personality need is **To Receive Nurturing** which they count on as a reward for volunteering. It's a costs versus rewards type of thing. Others may perceive their behavior as excessive but they consider it a tradeoff of necessity – at least – Or – at most – of quiet desperation.

We've been talking about people with a personality tendency and a personality need. Of course, as you probably surmised, people have more than one of each. It's safe to say we all have probably several of each. Those of us with a multifaceted personality may have such a diversity of characteristics, tendencies and needs that it becomes quite difficult to find a general factor around which this diversity can cluster. Some personality tendencies and needs complement each other – like a controlling tendency – and a need to care-give. Others seem to be each other's opposite – like a nurturing tendency and a need to be nurtured. Some seem to be so closely related they seem to be depicting the same thing – like a tendency to overlap relationships – and go to excessive lengths to obtain nurturance and support.

V. Full-Blown Personality Disorder – (Nature-Of)

I've been talking to you at great length about Axis II stuff – Personality Tendencies and Needs. I've also tried to show you how (as a therapist) I use what I perceive of the person's personality to shed light on what is going on with the person on Axis I [E.g. Social Anxiety; Axis I, Axis II – One preoccupied with being criticized or rejected in social situations]. There are cases, however, where my client, by their presentations and my clinical perceptions (which become the basis of my personality analysis) manifests an **enduring** pattern of person perception and self-experience and subsequent behavioral presentation – That – by virtue of the clustering of personality tendencies and needs around one specific dominant personality factor is pervasive and rigid – Has an onset in adolescence or early childhood – is persistent and resistant to change – And can eventually lead to impaired functioning.

We are now talking about a full-blown personality disorder – that differs from the Axis II stuff we priorly talked about – in that – then we spoke of personality tendencies and needs – Now we're talking about a **personality pattern** of person perception, self-experience, and behavioral presentation. These combine to produce (if you will) one dominant personality factor – Which, in turn, dominates the person's way of perceiving, experiencing, and behaving. [Cues that help me perceive the state or condition of the client's interpersonal functioning – Cues that help me perceive the client's level of impulse control.]

I'm sure the etiology of the personality is traceable to early childhood. The personality of the child developing through person perception and self-experience leads to personality tendencies, needs – which have the capacity to cluster eventually into one overall dominant personality factor. [This becomes both the subject and object of the client's perception and behavioral presentation (and the therapist's diagnosis). Quite often the person who I diagnose as having an Avoidant Personality Disorder is also experiencing High Anxiety – possibly having Panic Attacks – or, Depression (psychoneurotic rather than clinical). This one dominant personality factor around which the person's personality tendencies, needs, person perception, self-experience and presenting behaviors cluster gives name to the **Personality Type** one is talking about.]

VI. Avoidant Personality Disorder (APD)
For Our Paradigm

Let's use **Avoidant Personality Disorder** for our paradigm. Here's a surprise! – The dominant personality factor is **Avoidance**. Those clinicians which acknowledge the existence of personality disorders (many don't) diagnose them in persons in late adolescence or early adulthood at the earliest. [This isn't to suggest that they couldn't be present earlier in life, since our personality (at least in a rudimentary sense) is developed by age six.] Clinicians diagnose on the basis of what **Symptoms** the client presents. I call symptoms, **Perceptual Cues** – Cues that help me perceive the client's way of perceiving themselves – perceiving the way others perceive them – perceiving others. Cues that help me perceive the range, intensity, lability and appropriateness of their emotional response. That a person who I later diagnose as having an Avoidance Personality Disorder would present symptoms of anxiety and/or panic attacks would not surprise me in the least. The psychological defense a person relies upon to mitigate anxiety is avoidance. Heavy reliance upon this defense serves to reinforce personality tendencies and needs, person perceptions and self-experience, behavioral presentations – all geared to avoid. Remember, defenses are employed to preserve self-concept and alleviate anxiety.

How would a client having such a personality disorder present themselves perceptually? By their self-report – Which at first I would expect to be sparse – of few words – and those spoken haltingly. We're talking interpersonal contact here which the client has done their best to avoid whenever possible. So their anxiety level to start with will be high. They'll use their shell to protect themselves. The trade-off being – It keeps others out, but themselves in.

I'd work first then on establishing a safe, secure, non-threatening, nonjudgmental, caring, empathic, calm rapport with them – [Certainly, more support than anything resembling confrontation.] At some point relatively early in the therapeutic process, the client hopefully will start to open up to me and provide me with perceptual cues that help me identify their personality tendencies and needs. The client begins to share with me their perceptions of themselves – their perception of other's perception of them – and their perception of others. Perceptions of themselves refer to how they see themselves when they look at their self-concept. In an APD client – they wouldn't like most of what they see. [And remember – This is despite the work of their defenses to preserve their self-concept – Which in their case is preserving a picture of themselves that they are feeling (self-worth) is hardly worth saving.]

So for starters – a client with APD has a poor self-concept and low self-esteem. Their perception of their Self? – What do they see when they look at themselves? They see someone pretty much afraid of their own shadow. Someone who wished the floor would swallow them up when they were having what in their mind was significant interpersonal contact.

Someone reluctant to get even minimally involved with others unless early on they are certain of being liked. Someone who sees themselves socially as a fish out of water, at times their anxiety leaving them gasping for air. Afraid of any modicum of closeness for fear that the other upon closer scrutiny may find something that would bring them shame or ridicule. Someone obsessing with anticipatory thoughts that given the opportunity provided by their presence others might be critical of them, or even worse, reject them. Someone low on the take-a-chance scale, thinking negatively ahead that personal risks, new activities may prove embarrassing at best – at worst, humiliating. [The client need not present all of these perceptual cues. The number of them presented is not as relevant as is how extensively they fill the picture the client has of themselves.]

The question now that one needs to ask is – How did the client derive this picture of themselves in the first place? For the insights into the how, we go back to early childhood – When perceptions of oneself are first formed from – How the child perceives others perceiving them. About some things that happened in their past the APD client may not be forthcoming. Fallout from a traumatic event may have buried them – Memories too painful to remember – let alone talk about. But piecing perceptual cues together one can recreate a mosaic of happenings, interactions, situations, and the like – in which the client engaging in interpersonal contact (with significant others –

starting with parents, including some relatives, teachers, peers and friends) perceived these others perceiving them and responding to them with presentations of varying degrees of criticism, disapproval, displeasure, shaming and rejection. Varying degrees is to say they varied in intensity and frequency – But these responses over time accumulated sufficiently to form for the client a picture of Self – portraying mostly negativity.

The defensive maneuver most frequently chosen is to isolate oneself. To stay out of sight if possible. To keep to oneself as much as possible. To steer clear of and be ultra-careful not to agitate the punishing agent. The trade-off is perception of Self – when formed by perceptions of others perceiving them (that is mostly negative). The client is afraid to test the waters and perchance perceive a different perception of themselves from others – i.e. a positive response that could mitigate previous negativity. The result of which is a perception of Self that is self-perpetuated and is subsequently projected upon – and anticipated from – others they may have interpersonal contact with.

To put this more plainly, once the APD client has the negative self-concept – especially as it pertains to having interpersonal contact – and how poorly they have fared when they weren't able to avoid that contact – the defense of avoidance kicks in encouraging the client to avoid interpersonal contact whenever, wherever possible. The trade-off being an alleviation of anxiety and a preservation of the existing self-concept.

However, the cost of said defensive maneuver is isolation, aloneness, and severely limiting chances for closeness.

How does one help someone with APD? The treatment would be relevant in helping those with avoidant personality tendencies and needs as well. One can assume there's a conflict going on within the avoidant personality which is the culprit behind the anxiety. It could be an approach-avoidance conflict – meaning that the person has yearnings to get close but anticipatory fears of criticism, ridicule, rejection hold them back – creating a state of intense ambivalence. Or, it could be an avoidance-avoidance conflict – meaning the person finds being alone –

isolated from others with minimal interpersonal contact – overall a negative experience (albeit a less anxious one). However, anticipatory fears of criticism, ridicule, and rejection have a negative valence to them as well. So damned if they do – damned if they don't. An unenviable position to be in, to say the least.

The way a conflict gets resolved – and the anxiety it generates lessened – is to go one way or the other. Unfortunately the person with APD – or avoidant tendencies and needs – almost invariably goes the way of least resistance – Following the lead of their defense – Avoidance. Nothing ventured – nothing gained applies (and then it doesn't). The person "gains" relief from anxiety – when venturing nothing. However, what is "lost" – when nothing is ventured – is the chance to verify whether if the person were able to venture – would anything be gained. I think so – but the person thinks not.

I think it's appropriate at this point – before I go any further in discussing my treatment approach in dealing with APD and other personality disorders – to inform you that in my profession very, very few of my colleagues (in the general sense of the word) are willing or able to treat Personality Disorders. Maybe the advent of "Managed Care" has had something to do with the paucity of professionals willing or able to take this challenge on. Or, maybe it boils down to either they don't believe that Personality Disorders are a legitimate diagnostic category to treat – or, they lack the knowledge and experience to treat them. [Hey, maybe this is why as a provider I didn't get many referrals from "Managed Care"! Therapy for personality disorders can't be accomplished in "six easy sessions." It is slow going and long term.]

There are those who believe that personalities can't be changed. Some contend that the personality once developed remains essentially the same throughout one's life. I take exception to the above on two counts. "Once developed" makes me think of a point on a continuum and that's it. I contend that our personality continues to develop throughout our life. I believe in both **Personality Expansion** and **Personality Change**.

When I talk about **Personality Change** – I'm not talking about wholesale changes. I am talking about substantial modification, however. Throughout my thirty-five plus years of treating personality tendencies and needs, I have conceptualized these as a person having more, or less of, in their personality, and some yet to be discovered. So then when I perceive a person as having too much of a personality tendency or need, or too little of, or one yet to be discovered – the art of psychotherapeutic modification and discovery is about to begin.

Getting back to the treatment of an APD client or a client who has large avoidant tendencies in their personality – First and foremost they need support – [That's why I chose the name – Support Therapy Clinic]. For them to accept my support I have to earn their trust – Which in itself is no small thing – Since interpersonal contact is what they strive to avoid. Once I've got their trust – they start to open up to me (albeit somewhat guardedly – which I understand completely). By their presentation and the perceptual cues that come with it – I soon see from their perspective – How they see themselves – How they see others see them – How they see others. These perceptions of theirs have combined to give them the self-concept – the picture they have of themselves when they come to see me – a picture of inadequacy, inferiority, and overall self-negativity.

The goal is to help them change that picture from one perceived by the person overall – negative / to one perceived overall – positive. But more specifically, to change their picture of one who avoids interpersonal contact (if it's at all possible) / to one who realistically will not embrace it, but surely will feel more comfortable with it. I give them insights about themselves that may relate to past experiences they may have had when interacting with people – That it seems to me were based upon their personality and the other's brought to the situation. They perceived themselves and the other's perception of them, and the other, in such a subjective way, that I feel it necessary to revisit such experiences with them to give them my perception and interpretation. This then, hopefully, is a beginning for them to see things differently. Henceforth in treatment it will be an on-going exercise to validate their perceptions of them, of others – with mine. The therapeutic effect of this exercise is to challenge and, in some instances counter their past, and present, and future perceptions and interpretations which have, still do, and will (I hope less – counting on them to change) produce a negative self-concept.

Changing one's self-concept means changing the three facets of Person Perception – Ourselves, Others of ourselves, and Others. How does one change these person perceptions? By changing one's presentation. Presentation change is behavioral change. Perceptually one presents through appearance, mannerisms, gestures, facial expression, tone (how they say), content, (what they say). Back to my APD client. I help them think about themselves and feel about themselves differently – But the key to their changing their three facets of person perception is for them to do differently i.e. to **present** differently.

With my support behind them – they need to get out there – Which for them means interpersonal contact. The very suggestion of mine that they need to get out there brings on the anxiety. In time they'll discover that **Anticipatory Anxiety** is overrated by the avoidant personality – That the anxiety that surely comes when the direct contact occurs – isn't as high as anticipatory anxiety would lead them to believe – In fact – is lower than anticipatory anxiety.

There are two strategies for reducing the anxiety – preceding and during – interpersonal contact – One is called **Systematic Desensitization** (SD) – The other **Implosive Therapy**: Systematic Desensitization has the client test the waters (if you will) with their big toe (at first). Implosive Therapy has the client plunging in with their entire body – right off the bat – often referred to as the "Sink or Swim" method. [I acknowledge my bias in using SD – almost exclusively – in my practice and consequently will present a paradigm for SD only]

The idea behind SD is to have the client take on small doses of the noxious stimulus – In this case, interpersonal contact. For example . . . Have the client go to a social gathering, but set a time limit for themselves that they will stay there (in the social gathering's presence) even if they just observe and don't talk to anyone. Time's up, they leave . . . Next time they go again to a social gathering – again set a time limit (same as last time) only this time they try to talk to one person – time's up they leave . . .

Gradually, they work up to staying longer, but still set a time limit, and talk to two and then three and so on. The pattern is to alternate the lengthening of the time with increasing the number of people they talk to. [If the lengthening of the time and/or increasing the number of people they talk to at some point increases their anxiety level (anxiety which has been present all along – but they found manageable) – They may back up the time and number to a more manageable anxiety level.]

All of this is designed not to reduce the anxiety level to zero – Trust me, that's never going to happen. But it is intended to bring the anxiety down to a more comfortable level so they'll be able to put into practice the suggestions I have given them to increase their interpersonal skills. One suggestion I give that seems to work particularly well is – after my client has become proactive enough to present something like, Hi, I'm _____ and you? – Get the person to talk about themselves – Nine times out of ten, this breaks the ice – Trust me – Most people love to talk about themselves – and start to like the person who listens – That's you!

Regressive Behavior will occur now and then – The process is not a diagonally ascending line. I reassure my client telling them not to worry about a temporary anxiety glitch that momentarily got them off track. They're on their way. It would take a heck of a lot more than that to stop them. [So the client goes forward sharing their thoughts and feelings ad hoc with me. We rejoice over small victories together.]

Over time what's really happening is that my client is presenting themselves differently when interacting with others. They're becoming more comfortable in their skin. More self-assured. Liking the person they're bringing to the situation – (themselves, that is). Precipitating good feelings in the other about themselves – because they are willing and liking to listen to what the other has to say. The perception they are now getting from others of themselves is positive and that they're likeable. The perception they have of others is that they're positive and likeable. (I risk making this all sound too simplistic, but you get my drift.)

VII. Histrionic Personality Disorder (HPD)

We go next to the other end of the personality disorder spectrum. Having used APD as a prototype for how I approach, diagnose and treat personality disorders (PD), I will be more succinct with the other PD's I still wish to discuss with you. That being said, let me introduce you to the **Histrionic Personality Disorder**. [The diagnostic Manual mental health professionals use to diagnose PD refers to what these professionals observe in assessing clients as **Symptoms**. In adhering to my approach, diagnosis, and treatment of PD using my emphasis on personality, person perception, and self-experience as the tools of my profession – I use terms like personality tendencies and needs which give me **Perceptual Cues** upon their presentation. Using the four aspects of person perception and their self-report I give them a diagnosis and proceed with my strategy to help them.]

The HPD client presents overall a pervasive verbal and no-verbal behavioral pattern of over-the-top emotionality and attention-seeking. Personality tendencies and needs that they present include the following:

- Not a happy camper unless they're the center of attention.

- Sometimes to get their way may resort to sexually seductive or provocative behavior.

- Fickle and shallow in expressing their emotions.

Before I go on, I want you to take special notice of how the HPD client skillfully uses the four aspects of person perception to their exclusive advantage:

- Uses appearance (what we see of a person that does not move) to draw attention exclusively to themselves

- Their style of speaking (Voice Quality – their tone, inflection) (Voice Content – words used to impress – more than make sense)

- Self-dramatic, theatrical, exaggerated expression of emotion [Note: using the aspect of person perception – facial expression, gestures, mannerisms]

- As suggestible as they are suggestive

- Tends to overestimate the closeness they give and/or receive in a relationship

In treating the HPD client the first thing I want to do is help them change their presentation – starting with the way they present to me. They come in – as clients do – feeling anxious and apprehensive. Their defense is to do their shtick. They get into their routine [Which, of course, I see right through]. They'll test me for a couple of sessions – or so – and when they see I'm not buying, what they're selling – they start to settle down.

What they need most from me has already happened (although they may not as yet realize it). The HPD client needs most to have a relationship in which they feel comfortable and safe enough to lay down their shtick and reveal what's beneath the surface stuff. To be able to communicate normally – in a relatively calm and collected way – That's the kind of interactional experience they need to be a part of. The key, of course, is to help them get to the point where they are more in control of themselves – So they'll be able to stay on track despite the reality that someone other than I is on the other end of their interaction.

So, their therapy involves practicing realness rather than phoniness – with me – in their presentation. Anything short of realness I call them on and have them re-present it – authentically – this time. I want them to get in touch with their authentic Self – Which is starting to look better to them every day. Being their Real Self means helping them improve their self-concept and raise their self-esteem – So that their Self feels more and more at ease and comfortable with taking their Real Self on – Because they're growing into it.

VIII. Obsessive Compulsive Disorder (OCD)

Obsessive Compulsive Disorder is one of the toughest PD to treat. Perhaps one reason is because with OCD one is dealing with two major personality components – The way the person thinks and the way the person acts. Obsessions involve repetitive thoughts. Compulsions involve repetitive behaviors. It's really the content of their thoughts – i.e. what they obsess about – that gets them into cognitive, emotional and behavioral trouble. For some it can be just a word that is spoken that triggers their thoughts that follow – Which will not leave them alone. When they cannot control these thoughts – Make them stop, or go away – They get very anxious. Their need to control – what they can't control – creates the conflict within them – which then generates the anxiety.

The OCD client presents overall a pervasive pattern of preoccupation with orderliness, perfectionism, and mental and interpersonal control. The trade-off – i.e. the cost to their personality – is a substantial loss of flexibility, openness and efficiency.

Personality tendencies and needs that they present include the following:

- They get bogged down by the details that they ruminate over.

- As they work on a project, they have overly strict standards that from their perspective must be met (to satisfy their personality tendency towards perfectionism). If these self-imposed standards are not met they most likely will not complete the project.

- They have this image of themselves that their scruples, ethics, values must be beyond reproach, higher than the highest (culturally or religiously).

- Delegating tasks to others is torturous for them, because nobody can do the task as well as they can.

- They have a propensity for hanging onto things, objectively speaking – worn-out, worthless things – Add to this a miserly spending style fortified by the view that money is to be hoarded for future catastrophes. [An exception to this is the OCD who impulsively has to have what they see and doesn't compute the cost. Cfr – The OCD with impulsive trait.

- Rigidity and stubbornness are the pillars of the OCD person's personality profile.

Again in deciding how best to treat them – i.e. what approach and strategy to use – given the personality tendencies and needs they perceptually present – It becomes clear to me that the best thing I can do for them (at least at first) is to help them loosen up a bit in the way they treat themselves and others. They are too uptight. Too strict. Too hard on themselves. Everything for them is black or white. Either or. No in-between. So, as soon as I think they're ready – or even if they're not – I introduce them to the **gray in life** – a color with which they're unfamiliar. It's the gray in life that they've tried to color over with black or white. It's the gray in life (were they to use that color) that would heighten their anxiety.

Perceiving things as black or white makes living life so much easier.

However, other personality tendencies and needs make the obsessive-compulsive life extremely difficult – The repetitive thoughts usually on the dark and fearsome side – The broken record in the mind playing the thoughts over and over again. Some have found a way to cope – "Making a deal with the devil" (as it were) in that they find some "magical" behavior that transfers the preoccupation of the thoughts to concentration on the behavior. [Obviously this is no cure – At best it's a temporary remedy] [The compulsive one usually does well in the marketplace where mistake-free work is at a premium – Where if extra work needs to be done – task added to task – Give it to the compulsive one.]

Some OCD'ers are checkers – They can't leave the house without checking to see if all the burners are off on the stove. Before they get to their car they have to go back and recheck the stove. Some have to do this several times – and even then they may worry throughout the day. The way I try to help them help themselves is to teach them how to visualize their target – Study the picture of how the knobs (that turn each burner on) look when each burner's off – On many stoves they're straight up and down. Plant that picture firmly in their mind. Use that picture as their frame of reference when they are checking the burners to see that they're off before they leave the house. If what they see before their eyes matches the picture they have planted in their mind – trust their perception – and let it go. If they must – Recall the picture in their mind as they walk to their car – and let it go – For many, visualizing has been a godsend.

A word about the role compulsivity plays in a relationship. If a compulsive one hooks up with a dependent one – What you end up with is the compulsive one doing most of the work. The dependent one will complain to me that the compulsive one beats them to it – or wants it done right now. Or if the dependent finally gets going and does the job – the compulsive one follows not far behind correcting along the way. My insight to the compulsive one is to back off and try to restrain themselves from jumping in – Let the whole thing play itself out. To the dependent one – Become proactive.

Don't wait to be asked. Get in there and do the best job you can – As long as you're being honest with yourself, let the compulsive one do their follow-up thing (if they must) – But look at that as their thing and not a reflection on you.

IX. The Narcissistic Personality Disorder (NPD)

The **Narcissistic Personality Disorder** presents a pervasive thought and behavioral pattern featuring grandiosity, excessive need for admiration, and lack of empathy. They could stand all day before a mirror looking at themselves and not get bored – kissing themselves on the hand – whispering loving thoughts to themselves about themselves. You get the picture – Their picture.

One would hypothesize that the NPD would evolve from an early background of being excessively admired, singled out for praise. That this is how they became full of themselves. But interestingly enough, most of the NPD's I've treated evolved from an early background quite the opposite. They came from a childhood which was stark, stern, and strict. They yearned for attention but little was paid to them. No one in their family was really sensitive to what they were feeling – so they had no place to go with their feelings. Only their stuffed animals would listen to them. They were expected to practice cleanliness – to look as good as they could and not to cause any trouble. They became pleasers of others. They did and said the right things, but their feelings weren't in it.

They felt no love coming to them nor going out from them. Reality for them left them emotionally cold and aloof inside – even as outwardly they presented a pleasing appearance. It was in their fantasies that they tried to satisfy themselves – dreaming of someone coming along to love them and admire them. Believing their stuffed animals had feelings and loved them. Not feeling loveable because they had not felt loved – they tried in their fantasy life to feel love – In their own way – to love themselves. Unfortunately, it's a turn off for others who otherwise might be viable candidates to love them – To come across someone who ostensibly is in love with themselves. [The other not being able to look inside of them doesn't realize the love they feel for themselves is not real.]

The perceptual cues the NPD gives off in their presentation make it extremely hard for the perceiver to relate to them – let alone love them:

- Grandiose sense of self-importance

- Fantasies of unlimited success, across the board

- Believes that they are "special" – that only "special" people can see this –"ordinary" people can't

- Unrealistically (of course) believes only good things, favors, entitlements should come their way

- Will exploit you if given half a chance

- Wants more, so envies others – but also believes others envy them

- Shows arrogant, haughty behaviors or attitudes

- Lacks empathy – having received none – has none to give

The gap between the NPD's Ideal Self and Real Self is wide. Indeed, I treat them to help them narrow that gap. For them, their Ideal Self is the one they conjured up in their fantasies. Their Ideal Self is their Unreal Self. Their Real Self got lost in their childhood – buried beneath their fantasies and unreal self-love. I help them uncover their Real Self – which had they experienced real love from others – together with empathy – wouldn't have been buried so deeply. I give them the insight that by their "self-love" presentation – perceptually they are viewed as not needing the very things they seek – i.e. their "self-love" presentation is self-defeating. [Assertiveness holds one key – Sensitivity to what others are feeling holds the other. Assertiveness tempered with sensitivity will open the door to reciprocal caring – Being direct, open, and honest with their thoughts feelings, and needs – Being a good listener and caring empathizer help too.]

X. Borderline Personality Disorder (BPD)

Borderline Personality Disorder (Hands Down) has been the hardest one for me to treat. It's a multifaceted disorder. In some ways it is a collage of various other PD's – like HPD, APD, NPD, Dependent Personality Disorder DPD, et al. Key descriptive words for BPD would be frenetic, frantic, fluctuating, unstable, intense, impulsive, negative attention-seeking, self-destructive, etc:

- Emotional lability and instability – mood reactive

- Chronic feelings of emptiness – deadness inside

- In and out with anger – terrible temper – can and does get physical

- When over-stressed can become paranoid in their thinking – and to escape – temporarily dissociate.

The hardest thing to pin down with BPD is who is their Real Self. One gets glimpses of their Real Self –

albeit it's fragmented and not whole. The task is to build on those glimpses – To help them piece the fragments of their personality together. Looking at their self-concept, they and you (through them) see a shattered mirror reflecting back to them a Shattered Self. It's that Shattered Self they present to you.

Almost invariably theirs is a history of sexual abuse, psychological abuse, probably physical as well. Mixed messages. Double entendres aplenty. It was never given to them straight. Idealized one moment. Devalued the next. Never really knowing whether they and/or others were coming or going. Consumed by anger – It was the only feeling to fill their emptiness. Their impulsivity was expulsive, acting on and out their anger with reckless abandon. Punishing their body. Complicating their life by overindulging – Be it spending, sex, or substance.

How best to treat them? I'm still working on it! What I try to do for them is help them get grounded – And stay grounded as best they can when they're not with me. When I perceive them getting away from me in session – I work to bring them back and encourage them to refocus. The best I can offer them is a Now experience where at least one of us is reasonably healthy (that's me!). Even the slightest improvement in their ability to stay grounded interacting with me for the hour is a small victory (which, of course I reinforce).

One is constantly having to deal with **Transference** and **Counter Transference** issues in treating BPD's. Transference refers to the client transferring, projecting, if you will, their feelings onto the therapist. Counter Transference is the other way around from therapist to the BPD client. It's especially important that the therapist, above all, stays grounded.

XI. Antisocial Personality Disorder (AnPD)

For the sake of thoroughness, I'll include **Antisocial Personality Disorder** (AnPD to distinguish from APD – Avoidant). [I can't remember giving this diagnosis to any adult in my thirty-five years of practice] However, in my stint as a prison psychologist to the Men's Unit in the largest women's prison in Florida, it was another story. It was a medium security prison housing a population ranging from murderers to drug abusers. As one might have expected, AnPD was unfortunately a prevalent diagnosis – The perceptual cues revealing the personality tendencies and needs of AnPD are the following:

- Failure to conform to social norms with respect to lawful behaviors i.e. repeatedly performing acts that are grounds for arrest

- Deceitfulness: lying, using aliases, conning others

- Impulsivity – living in the moment, only for the moment

- Reckless disregard for own safety and other's

- Consistent irresponsibility

- Lack of remorse

Since I was the first psychologist in the Men's Unit prison history, I had no precedent to follow. That meant I could do my own thing as I saw fit. In the prison guards' minds my job was to pacify the inmates so that they would be less resistant to their control. Imagine the guard's surprise when I got their captain to allow me to meet with each one of them (guards, that is) one-on-one for "individual therapy."

I got out of my office and into the prison proper – walking and talking with inmates during their free time – (I admit – part of my humanistic bent.) Inmates are slow to trust authority figures [I don't blame them – From what I observed they had good reason.] It took a month and a half before I saw my first client in my office. He was a lifer who worked in the infirmary – I got to know because he took my daily blood pressure. Once he came in, the others followed – Despite the guards giving them a hard time when calling them out of line – "No. xxx – The shrink wants to see you."

I truly believe I was able to help some of them – If only to give them someone they could talk to outside of the guards and other inmates. I used my power of person perception to spot right away if they were "running a reel" on me. So they got as real as they could be with me under the circumstances. [The correctional officials knew that I could be objective about my clients – so I wasn't invited to the "Kangaroo Courts" they held.]

To show you the rapport over time I developed with many of the inmates – let me share with you one incident . . . I was called in one weekend to settle down one of the inmates who had gone berserk. Shortly after I arrived and was sizing up the situation trying to figure out what my first move would be – Guess what? – There was a prison break. Three escapees. The guards, and guns, and dogs followed. And I – I was left with a skeleton crew of guards, 250 inmates, one berserk inmate who I was working on settling down. Not only did I walk amongst the inmates unscathed, but they took turns over the hours watching over the troubled inmate so I could take breathers. I felt completely safe – An example to me of mutual trust.

I left the job after seven months. Let's just say the powers-that-be and I weren't on the same page – Heck not even in the same book – In our respective approaches to treating inmates. Their philosophy was contain and control. Mine was rehabilitate. I promised the inmates before I left, that I would do something for them when I got out. I did – and I'm glad I did. I got the largest newspaper in the area to publish my realistic, unadulterated perspective of that prison's life – Three articles, three days, front page. Inmates who couldn't read had it read to them. I kept my promise. Needless to say I was never able to use the prison officials as a personal or professional reference. (Ask me if I cared.)

XII. Wrapping Things Up

What I'm going to do now – to sort of wrap things up and put a bow on them – is to share with you for the first time in print a category of personality disorder I developed myself – spurred on by the perception that it kept showing up when I was assessing and diagnosing clients – especially male clients. It is a combination of **Dependent Personality Disorder** (DPD) (which I have saved for this moment) and **Passive Aggressive Personality Disorder** (PAPD), which is no longer part of the Diagnostic Manual. I call it **Hostile Dependent Personality Disorder (HoDPD).** Obviously, the two components of this personality disorder are **Hostility** and **Dependency**. The conceptualization behind this disorder is that in a relationship between a care-giver [i.e. a person with a large personality tendency to care-give] and a dependent [i.e. a person with a large personality tendency to be on the receiving end of that care] – This particular personality may manifest itself – showing up in the one – reinforced by the other – i.e.

showing up in the dependent one – reinforced by the care-giving one.

The relationship between the care-giver and care-receiver begins at birth – In most cases we're talking mother/child. The dependent personality begins – minus the hostility. The care-giving personality over time develops a controlling personality tendency. In a sense the care-giver becomes a care-taker – i.e. taking charge of – or control of – the dependent one. Both parents or parent substitutes may be involved by this time – but in most of the males I've treated, it's been – Mother.

The males in childhood and adolescence experience both the perception of themselves as dependent and controlled. Their perception of the other's perception of them is that they're dependent and controlled. Their perception of the other is that they depend on the other and are controlled by the other. Depending upon how the care-giving is presented (Here we're talking once again about appearance, facial expression, mannerisms, how they say, what they say) and how then it is perceived – the receiving one will either feel more closeness or control.

Herein lies the potential power, over the other, the care-giver has – To mete out: Just control. Control with closeness. Closeness with control. Just closeness. If dependency is relatively constant (as it is in some) and only control and closeness vacillate – the dependent one begins to perceive and feel more control than closeness. Control they will resent. Closeness they will turn away from. They will begin to perceive things in this way – That in order to get the closeness – they will have to live with the control!

Assuming similar contingencies of closeness and control play out in their adult relationship between the man and woman. Assuming also that it is more likely to be the man who is the dependent one and the woman the controlling care-giving one [It certainly could, or course, be the other way around] we could very well have a repeat situation – For the man whose dependency needs were met by a controlling mother – From his perspective he has traded one for the other – Unless perceptions, and personality tendencies change – resentment, anger can accumulate into hostility.

For this situation, couple therapy is the way to go. Seeing each individually, I'll likely discover the woman does not want to perceive herself (nor be perceived) as a controlling one. But, I then listen to the perceptions she has of the other – fitting the dependent personality profile. I talk to the man and basically crank him up – Push assertiveness, proactiveness. Show him how he's been reinforcing her controlling tendency with his inactiveness. I'm sure by now you're ahead of me in anticipating how well this works couple-wise [Better than you think – if each is willing to come away from the pole.]

XIII. As Far As You're Concerned

As you've been reading through these pages, I trust that you have tried to lower your defenses so that you might use the personality tendencies and needs I've alluded to [in describing perceptual cues to look for in these various personality disorders] to see if any, some, or many are pertinent for you. As you work your way through you may see one of your personality tendencies here – Another one – there. If perchance you find a number of them under one particular PD – Don't panic – Try to relax – You haven't been branded for life.

Approach personality tendencies you identify – scattered throughout (and those under one heading) in the same way. The operative word here is **Tendencies** – Whether scattered or grouped – they can be dealt with individually. Awareness – Lowering your defenses – Objectively, realistically, perceiving personality tendencies in yourself. [Check with your other whether they have perceived these in your presentation.]

Assuming you wish to modify some of these personality tendencies – Think of ways you can alter your presentation. [Hopefully, your other will have suggestions too.] Use the four aspects of person perception to effect change in your presentation. See a therapist if you choose to. This would give you support and insights to make the process of changing perceptions easier. Otherwise, observe others whose presentation is along the lines of what you want for yourself.

Practice the new presentations especially on those who don't already have a perceptual set of you from before. Presenting differently – you will perceive others perceiving you differently – And you'll perceive others differently. I'm hoping the "New You" will be someone closer to the "Real You" – Both to yourself as you perceive yourself – And to others to whom you present yourself.

Blessings
Take Good Care,
Doc Ken
K. L. Fischer, PhD

WE'VE GOT PERSONALITY – NOW WHAT!

About the Author

☐ Dr. Kenneth L. Fischer (affectionately called Doc Ken) has been in helping professions his entire adult life.

☐ Founder and pastor of Peace Lutheran Church, Disco, MI

☐ Pastor of Mt. Olive Lutheran Church, Grand Rapids, MI

☐ Junior High School teacher 8th grade English, 9th grade Latin, Muskego, MI

☐ First psychologist in the history of the Men's Unit, State Prison, Lowell, FL

☐ Dr. Fischer received his PhD in Personality Psychology, Michigan State University, East Lansing, MI

☐ His doctoral work was in Person Perception

☐ An instructor and lecturer, Dept. of Psychology, University of Wisconsin, Milwaukee, WI

☐ Also taught at various colleges throughout the Milwaukee-Metro area, namely Milwaukee Area Technical College, Mt. Mary College, Alverno College, and at Carthage College, Racine, WI

☐ Dr. Fischer has been a practicing psychologist in his own clinic for the past thirty-five years, treating adult couples and individuals

- [ ] His areas of expertise are in Personality and Person Perception

- [ ] His specialty is Personality Disorders

- [ ] Support Therapy Clinic is located in Hartland, WI

Other Books by Kenneth L. Fischer, PhD

Closeness Without Control:
The Key To A Loving Reciprocal Relationship Of
Assertive Independent Equals

Seeing Ourselves As We See Others See Us:
Our Personality Develops Through Person Perception
and Self-Experience

The Gray Area Of Psychological Abuse:
Abusee? Abuser? Or Both? How Can We Tell?
What Can We Do?

Psychologically Speaking What Are We Really Saying?
The Music Behind The Music Behind Our Words

Don't Like The Way It Is - Change It:
Changing Before Or After An Ultimatum

Don't Be A Stranger (To Yourself):
Go Outside Yourself To Get Inside Yourself Then Turn
Yourself Inside Out

The Art And Efficacy Of Managing Person Perceptions:
Manipulation In Its Highest Psychotherapeutic Sense

In Defense Of Defensiveness:
Knowing Our Defenses, Lowering Our Defenses,
Living With Our Defenses

The Incomparable Spunkerface and Company:
Heaven Sent - Heaven Bent

Lamenting The Loss of Loyalty:
Where Has All The Loyalty Gone?!